ABIGAIL ADAMS

From the Revolution to the White House

Tamara Orr Staats

Boston, Massachusetts
Chandler, Arizona
Glenview, Illinois
Upper Saddle River, New Jersey

Illustrations
Opener, 1, 2, 4, 5, 6, 10, 12, 14 Norbert Sipos.

Photographs
Every effort has been made to secure permission and provide appropriate credit for photographic material. The publisher deeply regrets any omission and pledges to correct errors called to its attention in subsequent editions.

Unless otherwise acknowledged, all photographs are the property of Pearson Education, Inc.

Photo locators denoted as follows: Top (T), Center (C), Bottom (B), Left (L), Right (R), Background (Bkgd)

3 Prints and Photographs Division, LC-DIG-ppmsca-15705/Library of Congress; 7 Detroit Publishing Company Photograph Collection, Prints and Photographs Division, LC-D4-17010/Library of Congress; 8 Prints and Photographs Division, LC-USZ62-55196/Library of Congress; 9 Prints and Photographs Division, LC-USZC2-2243/ Library of Congress; 11 Prints and Photographs Division, LC-USZC4-4970/Library of Congress; 13 Prints and Photographs Division, LC-USZC2-2645/ Library of Congress; 15 Prints and Photographs Division, LC-USZ62-10016/Library of Congress.

ISBN-13: 978-0-328-67639-2
ISBN-10: 0-328-67639-X

3 4 5 6 7 8 9 10 V0FL 15 14 13 12

A Remarkable Woman

Abigail Adams lived at a time when women had little hope of changing the world. In the 1700s women did not get much education. They could not run for office or vote. If they were married, they could not own property.

Abigail Adams and other women of her time had very few choices about how they would live their lives. They were expected to get married, have children, and take care of their families.

Despite these limits, Abigail Adams is remembered today for her strong opinions and her **influence** on two presidents. She helped shape history by advising her husband, John Adams, the second president of the United States. She also influenced her son, John Quincy Adams, who became our sixth president.

Abigail Adams wrote hundreds of letters during her lifetime. They show her opinions and give us a fascinating look at what life was like during the country's important early events. They also show how close she was to her husband, John Adams.

John Adams

Growing Up

Abigail Adams was born Abigail Smith on November 11, 1744, in Weymouth, Massachusetts. She was the second of four children. Abigail's father, William Smith, served as the minister in Weymouth.

The Smith home was comfortable and happy, and Reverend Smith was a kind and loving father. On most days, when she wasn't doing her chores, Abigail Smith would likely have been found in her father's library reading a book.

Abigail Adams's birthplace

Education

As was the custom of the time, Abigail Smith was taught at home by her mother. William Smith wanted all of his children to share his love of learning, even his girls. Abigail Smith had the use of his library and studied as many subjects as she could.

Even though she read many books, Abigail Adams had poor spelling and grammar that always embarrassed her. Abigail Adams always wished she could have gone to school as boys did. She felt it was very unfair that girls were not given the same education as boys.

John Adams

In 1762, a young lawyer named John Adams began spending time with Abigail Smith. They fell deeply in love. The couple lived only five miles from each other and saw each other often. They also wrote many letters to each other.

The letters of both were filled with warmth and respect. For Abigail, writing letters was a way to express her thoughts and feelings. She once wrote, "My pen is always freer than my tongue. I have wrote many things to you that I suppose I never could have talked."

Marriage

Abigail Smith and John Adams were married on October 25, 1764. The couple settled at John Adam's childhood home in Braintree, Massachusetts. It was the beginning of a partnership that would last 54 years.

It was not long before John Adams became a very important leader in the American **colonies**, which were ruled by Great Britain. Because of his work, the two were apart for months or even years at a time. During their lives, they wrote hundreds of letters to stay in touch.

John Adams was born in this house in 1735.

Boston

In 1768, the Adamses moved to Boston to be nearer to John Adams's work. Abigail Adams loved city life. She was kept busy raising her growing family. In Boston she had lots of interesting visitors and plenty to talk about.

The colonists in Boston were becoming unhappy with British taxes. Some were even talking about **independence** from Britain.

On March 5, 1770, British troops fired on an angry crowd. Several people were killed. John Adams did not agree with the taxes either, but he defended the British soldiers at their trial. Many people were outraged. But John Adams believed that everyone had a right to a fair trial. Abigail Adams supported him through this very difficult time.

British troops opened fire on a mob of colonists in Boston. The incident became known as the Boston Massacre.

John Adams (far right) served on a committee to write the Declaration of Independence.

Off to Philadelphia

Tensions grew. It looked like the colonists would have to fight a war to win their independence from Britain. The leaders decided to hold a meeting, called the Continental Congress, in Philadelphia. John Adams was chosen as a **delegate** to Congress. He left for Philadelphia in 1774.

Abigail Adams knew it was John Adams's duty to go to Philadelphia. But she missed him terribly while he was gone.

Abigail Adams managed the farm while her husband was away.

Apart

While John Adams was away, Abigail Adams moved back to the farm in Braintree. What did a wife of the 1770s do when her husband was away? In Abigail Adam's case, nearly everything. She hired and managed workers, tended the crops, and milked the cows twice each day. She paid the bills, and took care of the family, now four children. She did all this without dishwashers, laundry machines, or frozen foods.

During this time apart, Abigail and John Adams continued to exchange letters. She told him the news from the Boston area. Many of the colonists were **boycotting**, or refusing to buy, British goods. This meant many supplies such as candles, lamp oil, tea, and coffee were hard to get.

In April 1775, the first battle of the American Revolution was fought in the village of Lexington, Massachusetts. This was just 20 miles away from Braintree. And when colonists fought the British a month later on Breed's Hill north of Boston, Abigail and eight-year-old John Quincy raced to the top of a nearby hill. They could see the flashes of fire and smoke from the battle.

Besides telling her husband the news in her letters, Abigail Adams expressed her opinions. One of her most famous letters was dated March 31, 1776. She encouraged her husband and the other Congress delegates to "remember the ladies" when they wrote new laws. She warned, "Do not put such unlimited power into the hands of the husbands."

In one of her letters, Abigail Adams told how she watched a battle from a hill in Braintree.

Speaking Out

Abigail did not just argue for women's rights. She also felt strongly that **slavery**, which was then practiced in the colonies, was wrong. "It always appeared a most evil scheme to me," she wrote. How could some Americans fight for freedom when they enslaved other people? "We are daily robbing and stealing from those who have as good a right to freedom as we have."

George Washington was sworn in as president. John Adams stands at his left.

A New Country

Congress declared independence from Britain on July 4, 1776. Later, Congress sent John Adams to France to talk with leaders there. He took their oldest son, John Quincy, with him. It was very hard for Abigail Adams to let them go. If British ships had caught John Adams, he could have been hanged for **treason**. Once again, Abigail Adams was left alone to manage the farm. She knew her **sacrifice** was necessary for the cause of freedom.

The Americans won the war in 1783. Adams continued to serve the young United States, first as vice president, then as president himself. He continued to rely on Abigail Adams's advice. In 1797, when he became president of the United States, he wrote her, "I never wanted your advice and assistance more in my life."

Mrs. President

We know from John Adams's letters how much he valued his wife's advice. However, many people did not feel the same way. Some of President Adams's rivals called Abigail Adams "Mrs. President." They felt she had too much influence over his decisions. Abigail Adams saw no reason not to advise her husband as she had always done.

The Adamses were the first family to live in the White House. It was not quite finished when they moved in.

Home at Last

After John Adams's time as president was over, the couple returned to their farm. At last they had time together. Abigail Adams continued to write many letters. She often gave advice to her son, John Quincy.

On October 28, 1818, Abigail Adams died of typhoid fever. She and John Adams had shared 54 years of marriage. After she died he said, "I wish I could lay down beside her and die, too."

For the sake of her country, Abigail Adams had made many sacrifices. She served with courage in many ways. She used her pen to speak out for women's rights and against slavery. She used her brilliant mind to help shape our country's history and to make a difference.

Glossary

boycott to refuse to do business with a company or country

colony a place ruled by another country

delegate a person chosen to speak for others

independence freedom from the rule of another country

influence the ability to have an effect on others

sacrifice something given up

slavery forcing people to work without pay and without freedom

treason the act of being a traitor to one's country